Obstacles to
Deliverance

THE FRANK HAMMOND BOOKLET SERIES

FRANK HAMMOND

OBSTACLES TO DELIVERANCE:
WHY DELIVERANCE SOMETIMES FAILS
by Frank Hammond
ISBN 10: 0-89228-203-7
ISBN 13: 978-089228-203-6

Copyright © 2002. Revised 2011
Impact Christian Books

Impact Christian Books, Inc.
332 Leffingwell Ave., Suite 101
Kirkwood, MO 63122
(314) 822-3309

www.impactchristianbooks.com

All passages are from the KING JAMES BIBLE unless otherwise noted.

Printed in the United States of America

PART I

WHY DELIVERANCE SOMETIMES FAILS

Why does deliverance sometimes fail? In answering this question, several things must be taken into account. This is, in essence, the same question raised by Jesus' first disciples. When these disciples were unable to cast out a *spirit of epilepsy*, they were puzzled and asked Jesus the reason for their failure. Jesus gave a multi-part answer which leads us to take into account the petitioner's faith, the deliverance minister's capability, the spiritual qualifications that must be met, the strength of the spirit confronted and the strategy of warfare employed. First, let us consider the importance of faith.

LACK OF FAITH

The father of an epileptic boy complained to Jesus,

> "I BROUGHT HIM TO YOUR DISCIPLES, BUT THEY COULD NOT CURE HIM."
>
> MATT. 17:16

To which Jesus replied, "O faithless and perverse generation..." (Matt. 17:17). The word generation (*genea*) means "race" and refers to the Jewish people who, for the most part, refused to believe Jesus was the Messiah. Jesus was identifying the father of the epileptic son as part of that *faithless and perverse generation.* In Mark's account, the context reveals that the unbelieving scribes were disputing with the disciples over their failure to cast the deaf and dumb spirit out of the boy (Mark 9:14-17). The disciples were surrounded by an unbelieving multitude.

The unbelieving father besought Jesus, "If You can do anything, have compassion on us and help us" (Mark 9:22). Jesus answered the unbelieving father,

> "IF THOU CANST BELIEVE, ALL THINGS ARE POSSIBLE TO HIM THAT BELIEVETH."
>
> MARK 9:23

Thus, Jesus was showing that the disciples' failure was due to the unbelief of the one seeking deliverance. Jesus had encountered the same problem in Nazareth where...

> "HE DID NOT DO MANY MIGHTY WORKS THERE BECAUSE OF THEIR UNBELIEF."
>
> MATT. 13:58

When confronted over his unbelief,

> "THE FATHER OF THE CHILD CRIED OUT AND SAID WITH TEARS, 'LORD, I BELIEVE; HELP MY UNBELIEF!'"
>
> MARK 9:24

Whereupon Jesus rebuked the unclean spirit, and it came out.

Another parent who came to Jesus for a child's deliverance was the Syrophonecian mother. Jesus refused her request for deliverance until she expressed faith, whereupon Jesus said,

> "O WOMAN, GREAT IS THY FAITH: BE IT UNTO THEE EVEN AS THOU WILT. AND HER DAUGHTER WAS MADE WHOLE FROM THAT VERY HOUR."
>
> MATT. 15:28

Jesus had given His disciples absolute authority to cast out all demons:

> "THEN HE CALLED HIS TWELVE DISCIPLES TOGETHER AND GAVE THEM POWER AND AUTHORITY OVER ALL DEMONS."
>
> LUKE 9:1

How could they fail? The twelve failed because they had been influenced by the "*unbelieving and perverse generation*" and had lost their own faith to cast out demons. Therefore, Jesus addressed His disciples directly on the importance of faith, explaining their inability to cast out the demon:

> "BECAUSE OF YOUR UNBELIEF: FOR VERILY I SAY UNTO YOU, IF YE HAVE FAITH AS A GRAIN OF MUSTARD SEED, YE SHALL SAY UNTO THIS MOUNTAIN, REMOVE HENCE TO YONDER PLACE; AND IT SHALL BE REMOVED; AND NOTHING SHALL BE IMPOSSIBLE UNTO YOU."
>
> MATT. 17:20

It is important that both petitioner and minister have faith that when a spirit is commanded to go in the name of Jesus, it must go. Authority to cast out demons is contingent upon *faith*. Both God and demons know whether active faith is present. A teaching or instructional time that precedes deliverance provides an opportunity to build faith. Jesus did not tell His disciples that their faith must be gigantic. A mustard seed-sized of faith is sufficient so long as it is genuine faith.

LACK OF SPIRITUAL DISCIPLINE

Let us also consider the capability and qualification of the deliverance minister. Jesus also said,

"THIS KIND CAN COME OUT BY NOTHING BUT PRAYER AND FASTING."

MARK 9:29

The NU Greek New Testament omits "fasting." We know at this time the disciples of Jesus were not required to fast. When the scribes and Pharisees brought this up, Jesus explained,

"CAN YOU MAKE THE FRIENDS OF THE BRIDEGROOM FAST WHILE THE BRIDEGROOM IS WITH THEM? BUT THE DAYS WILL COME WHEN THE BRIDEGROOM WILL BE TAKEN AWAY FROM THEM; THEN THEY WILL FAST IN THOSE DAYS."

LUKE 5:34–35

Jesus, our Bridegroom, is not with us now, so prayer and fasting are spiritual prerequisites for successful encounters with demons. The deliverance minister must be a man of prayer and fasting; not a ritual prayer but a life of personal prayer accompanied by fasting. This is not a requirement that the deliverance minister fast before every deliverance situation, otherwise those who minister deliverance daily would be on a perpetual fast. A spiritually disciplined person is needed; one who is strong in prayer and has a fasting life-style. These two spiritual disciplines equip a minister and insure the anointing necessary for effective ministry!

VARYING STRENGTH OF DEMONS

Notice that Jesus made a distinction between spirits. "This kind" indicates that some demons are stronger and more determined than others, and we have found this to be a certainty. Demons are personalities, and just as some people have stronger wills than others, so it is with demons. We are commissioned to "wrestle" against Satan's host, and most wrestling contests are not won in a flash. Wrestling denotes putting pressure on the enemy until he is conquered. Failure can result from the deliverance minister giving up rather than pressing through.

CONDITIONS NOT MET

The candidate for deliverance must meet certain criteria:

1. FORGIVENESS

He must forgive all who have trespassed against him, otherwise, he is "turned over to the tormentors" (Matt. 18:35), and he cannot be liberated until he has met God's condition to forgive.

2. REPENTANCE

He must repent of all sin. Repentance is the prelude to deliverance. I recall a deliverance case where a man refused to confess homosexuality as a sin. He could not receive deliverance because he held on to this particular sin. Another example is the sin of abortion, which must be confessed as a sin of murder.

3. OCCULT OBJECTS

He must destroy all paraphernalia that give demons a legal right. Deliverance can be blocked by ungodly things a person possesses. We were unsuccessful in ministering deliverance to a gentleman when the Lord called my attention to a Masonic ring he was wearing. Acting on the explanation that I gave him as to the ring's demonic ties, he agreed to remove the ring. The moment he slipped the ring from his finger the demons began to come out of him. As deliverance was taking place through Paul's ministry in Corinth, "Many of them also which used curious arts brought their books together, and burned them before all men" (Acts 19:19). One must be willing to renounce and destroy all cult, occult and idolatrous books and paraphernalia in his possession.

4. PRIOR INVOLVEMENT IN OCCULT & FALSE RELIGIONS

He must renounce and ask God's forgiveness for all involvement in idolatry, the occult, cults and Eastern Religion (including the martial arts and Yoga exercises which cannot be separated from heathen religious connections).

5. DESIRE TO BE DELIVERED

He must want deliverance. "Whoever calls upon the name of Lord shall be delivered" (Joel 2:32). Oddly enough, there are some who prefer bondage to deliverance. Some have descended into mental illness as an escape from the memories of abuse and other traumas, and others have chosen to escape the responsibilities of life. For example, they may be institutionalized, and there they are housed, fed and clothed and others care for their every need. Should they be delivered they would have to go to work and provide for themselves. To some, this is an unacceptable option.

Another common escape is into childishness. There will be a "little boy" or "little girl" spirit that locks the individual into childish behavior. Behind this escape is the fear of growing up with its resultant responsibilities.

Still others relish the attention they are getting through receiving deliverance ministry. Such individuals will never admit to a breakthrough. They will always require additional deliverance because it is a special time of getting attention which they have heretofore lacked.

PASSIVITY

Some deliverance attempts end in failure because the counselee is passive. This can be due to tranquilizing drugs that render the individual from getting his will involved in the ministry. It is very important for the one seeking deliverance to have his will involved. When medications are found to be a barrier, it may be necessary to have that person taper off his medications — under the advice of a doctor — and come back for deliverance at a later time. Suspension of medications is a short-time requirement to facilitate deliverance. If a doctor has prescribed tranquilizing drugs, let the doctor decide that this person does not require them any longer.

In some cases, the person's will power is weak. He has never adequately strengthened his will in making life-changing choices. He needs to be taught and required to take a stand. Lead him to vocalize confessions and prayers of deliverance. Have him declare his appropriation of God's promises and command demons to go. Such activation of the will is in keeping with the Word of God which declares,

"SUBMIT TO GOD. RESIST THE DEVIL AND HE WILL FLEE FROM YOU."

JAS. 4:7

Unteachable

Occasionally, there will be an individual who challenges the deliverance minister's authority and counsel. He intends to make the minister think that the minister is the one with a problem rather than himself. A basic requirement for receiving deliverance is a teachable spirit. A deliverance minister functions like a spiritual doctor. It is his job to diagnose the problem and then prescribe God's remedy. He is unable to perform the spiritual "surgery" of removing the troubling demons without the counselee's cooperation.

Control

Then there is the case of the one seeking deliverance having his own agenda. If he is to receive help it must be on his own terms. He comes in with his own need diagnosed and dictates his conditions for receiving help. This control attitude will abort a ministry. The minister who is dependent upon the leading of the Holy Spirit cannot be hamstrung by the counselee's desire to control what and how deliverance takes place.

Self Deception

Self-deception is one of the most powerful of strongholds. It is a basic compensation for inferiority. The devil offers a false sense of importance to those who have been rejected and feel of less value in comparison to others. They are deceived into believing that for one reason or another they have found something of worth to which they can cling. This "something" may be a doctrine, a ministry gift, a revelation or a guidance technique...

"A person will cling to a deception because it appears valuable. It seems to offer security, recognition, acceptance, approval or love. Since the deception seems so important, it is stoutly defended. When the deception is challenged, the person feels threatened. He becomes determined that no one will take away the one thing that makes him feel important or secure. Therefore, he had rather suffer persecution than give up his deception. Only by the grace of God will the seriously self-deceived person escape his bondage."[1]

Not Understanding How Satan's Kingdom Functions

One must take into account that in deliverance we are not dealing with spirits singly but with a network or kingdom of spirits. This truth is found in the word "principalities" (Eph. 6:12), which signifies spirits working together in rank as a company of soldiers.

Scripture also reminds us that Satan's kingdom is not divided:

"AND IF SATAN CAST OUT SATAN, HE IS DIVIDED AGAINST HIMSELF; HOW THEN SHALL HIS KINGDOM STAND?"

MATT. 12:26

[1] See *Overcoming Rejection*, Chapter 5, by Frank Hammond. Available at www.impactchristianbooks.com

If Satan's kingdom is not divided then it is unified; unified by a common propensity to evil. Also, the ruler spirit must be subdued. Jesus demonstrated the priority of dealing with "the strong man."

> "OR ELSE HOW CAN ONE ENTER INTO A STRONG MAN'S HOUSE, AND SPOIL HIS GOODS, EXCEPT HE FIRST BIND THE STRONG MAN? AND THEN HE WILL SPOIL HIS HOUSE."
>
> MATT. 12:29

FAILURE TO SEEK THE LORD'S BATTLE PLAN

We might conjecture that the disciples had fallen into a pattern of deliverance, relying upon previously discovered methods to deal with demons. If this was the case, it was an unfortunate mistake often made by deliverance workers. In each deliverance situation we need to seek the Holy Spirit's battle strategy. It is best to approach each case as different, remaining flexible to the Spirit's leading. Allow Him to set the battle plan. Let Him tell you where to begin, how to proceed, and when and how to terminate each session.

LACK OF KNOWLEDGE CONCERNING DELIVERANCE

The deliverance minister's knowledge of deliverance, gained from Spirit-taught Bible revelation, is the basis for successful deliverance. Some of our first attempts at deliverance were failures. Although we had zeal it was not according to knowledge. For example, we did not realize that a person could have more than one spirit. We were gullible in believing what spirits spoke through a person, as when one spirit announced, "If Jesus were here, I would have to leave. But He is not here." Instead of rebuking the lying spirit, we pled for Jesus to return!

> "ALL SCRIPTURE IS GIVEN BY INSPIRATION OF GOD... THAT THE MAN OF GOD MAY BE ... THOROUGHLY FURNISHED UNTO ALL GOOD WORKS."
>
> 2 TIM. 3:16-17

LEARNING FROM OUR FAILURES

The disciples were genuinely concerned over their failure to cast out the *epileptic spirit*, so they did a very wise thing: they turned to Jesus for help. We, too, should be very concerned when we encounter deliverance failures. We need to know "why?" After all, Jesus has given us power and authority over all demons just as He did the twelve apostles (Luke 9:1) and the seventy disciples (Luke 10:19). We must remain humble and teachable. Was the failure due to some lack on the minister's part, or was it due to some unmet condition by the one ministered unto? When there is failure for any reason, we must go to Jesus for His assessment.

Each person is important, and his deliverance need is legitimate. We want to be at our very best so that every captive will be set free. We are dealing with the lives of those for whom Christ laid down His life.

If the fault lies with the deliverance minister, he must find the reason and correct it. If the failure is on the part of the deliverance seeker, he needs all the help he can get and is willing to receive. We cannot settle for partial success but must press on to full potential.

PART II

OBSTACLES TO DELIVERANCE

QUESTIONS
IN THE
MIND OF MAN

So far, we have covered the topic of why deliverance sometimes fails. It is worth concentrating further on one particular block to the deliverance ministry — the *mind* and *theology* of man.

There are myths, misunderstandings and misinformation concerning the ministry of deliverance. The first battleground is in the minds of men, where Satan has sown questions, doubts and fears that become hindrances to involvement in this valid, biblical ministry.

We need not spend time with those who are unteachable and argumentative. Jesus sometimes gave a simple, straightforward answer to His critics, but spent His time ministering to the people who were receptive and teaching His disciples. We will do well to follow His example.

Those who want an answer should be given an answer. Ignorance, prejudice and fear are hurdles that some sincere Christians must get over before they are willing to become involved in spiritual warfare. We must teach those who are receptive.

The only way to deal with the devil and demons is through direct confrontation. Furthermore, God has given the Christian and His Church the commission to cast out demons (see Matthew 10:1; Luke 10:17–19; Mark 16:17). Some believers have false opinions that prevent them from accepting deliverance as a vital ministry. Before one can bring himself to obedience to deal with the devil and demons, the following obstacles must be overcome in one's mind.

OBSTACLE 1
FEAR AND TERROR AT THE MENTION OF DEMONS, THE DEVIL OR DELIVERANCE

THE TRUTH...

The perceptions of demons held by many have been taken from fiction, mythology and superstition rather than from Scripture. The fear that some have of deliverance has been fostered in part through such films as *The Exorcist* and *Rosemary's Baby*, which are designed to create mystery, sensationalism, violence and fear rather than to convey truth.

The Christian should look at his resources and know that he is stronger than the enemy. Light dispels darkness. Fear and terror will leave when people embrace the truth. Faith overcomes fear (Rom. 10:17).

OBSTACLE 2
UNBELIEF: THERE IS NO SUCH THING AS THE DEVIL OR DEMONS

THE TRUTH...

Wrong concepts of the devil have been programmed by the world. He is not running around in a red suit with a pitchfork. He is not the ruler over hell. One day he will become the chief prisoner in hell (Rev. 20:10).

The Bible is filled with truth about Satan and demon spirits. Jesus said, "Ye shall know the truth, and the truth will make you free" (John 8:32). If we expect to be free we must know the truth about the devil. The Bible is the basis for our beliefs.

When Jesus spoke about demons He was not, as some contend, accommodating Himself to the opinion of men or the culture of the day. The Word of God is true. Demons exist.

OBSTACLE 3
DEMONS ARE REAL, BUT TOO POWERFUL FOR US TO CONFRONT

THE TRUTH...

We must not think that the devil is void of power and weapons, yet we must not think of him as having unlimited access into our lives.

The devil can do no more than he is allowed to do. He must work through accusation, deception and temptation.

Jesus defeated Satan through the cross and the resurrection. We are seated with Christ and have power over the devil (Eph. 1:18-2:7).

As believers in Christ, we have complete power over the devil and his demons. We can tread upon them and they are powerless to retaliate (Luke 9:1; 10:19).

OBSTACLE 4
DELIVERANCE IS VALID;
HOWEVER, IT SHOULD BE LEFT TO THE EXPERTS

THE TRUTH...

Who exactly is an expert? We agree that a Christian should have knowledge of demons and deliverance. If one thinks deliverance is for experts then he should become one! Jesus expects all believers to cast out demons (Matt. 12:30).

Christ's commission is given to the Church. Mark 16:17 says that those who believe *shall cast out demons*. Deliverance is a part of the Gospel of salvation that is for the whole man — spirit, soul and body. Casting out demons is a simple, basic sign that should accompany the ministry of witnessing believers (Mark 16:15,17).

OBSTACLE 5
CHRISTIANS CANNOT HAVE DEMONS

THE TRUTH...

In the Bible no distinction is made between believers and unbelievers having demons. The reason: both alike can have demons.

Deliverance is called "the children's bread" (Matt. 15:21-28; Mark 7:24-30), which means it is for God's own sons and daughters; purchased by the blood of Jesus. Therefore, a distinction is made as to who is qualified for deliverance. It is for God's children – for believers.

When demons are cast out of a person, the "house" must be filled (Matt. 12:43-45). How could an unbeliever fill his house? He is void of spiritual resources. Therefore deliverance is *only* meant to be ministered to the Christian.

The Christian is a *temple of the Holy Spirit* (1 Cor. 6:19). Believers in the New Covenant are likened to the Temple under the Old Covenant. A quick look at the Temple in Jerusalem unlocks the rich meaning behind this metaphor...

> There were three areas to the Temple, and there are three areas in us. Body, soul and spirit are parallel to the Outer Court, the Holy Place and the Holy of Holies. When the Temple was dedicated, God's presence indwelled the Holy of Holies. When we are saved, our spirit is quickened and indwelled by God. Thus Jesus sets up His throne in our spirit – our personal Holy of Holies.

> And yet, even though God's presence filled the Holy of Holies in the Old Testament, Jesus still had to cleanse the temple during His earthly ministry. He "cast out" all that defiled it.

> However, note that only the outer court needed cleansing. It had become a "den of thieves" (Matt. 21:13). God's presence was still undisturbed and reigning in His Temple — in the Holy of Holies.

According to Matt. 8:16–17, *deliverance* and *healing* are provisions of Christ's atoning blood. This means they were part of what Jesus was accomplishing on the cross, the same cross where we also receive our eternal salvation. The benefits of the cross are for those who accept the work of the cross.

WHEN EVENING CAME, MANY WHO WERE DEMON-POSSESSED WERE
BROUGHT TO HIM, AND HE DROVE OUT THE SPIRITS WITH A WORD
AND HEALED ALL THE SICK. THIS WAS TO FULFILL WHAT WAS SPOKEN
THROUGH THE PROPHET ISAIAH:

"HE TOOK UP OUR INFIRMITIES
AND BORE OUR DISEASES."

MATT. 8:16–17

Likewise, if it were impossible for a Christian to have a demon, then neither could he become sick, for both *healing* and *deliverance* are benefits of the cross (Matt. 8:16–17).

Logic tells us that it is better to acknowledge that you have a demon (if you do), and cast it out rather than deny you have a demon and keep it. Whatever torments you is most likely rooted in some form of demonic bondage.

We also learn in 2 Cor. 10:3-5, a verse addressed to Christians, that we can have "strongholds" in our minds. These are the devil's strongholds. The remedy requires spiritual weapons to pull down the devil's strongholds.

Also in Second Corinthians is a warning to Christians that it is possible to "receive another spirit" other than the Holy Spirit (2 Cor. 11:4).

OBSTACLE 6

DEMONS HAVE NO ACTIVITY IN CIVILIZED COUNTRIES

THE TRUTH...

This obstacle lies in the belief that demons are active only in remote countries where witchcraft and idolatry prevail.

It is true that demonic activity is intense in countries where witchcraft and idolatry prevail. However, witchcraft and the occult have made great inroads into all civilized countries.

There are many possible ways to expose oneself to demons other than through witchcraft and the occult. This is one of Satan's deceptions: as long as one thinks he is too intelligent or cultured to be demonized, he is blind to how demons gain entrance and how they function. There are demons in every culture.

OBSTACLE 7
DEMONS WILL COME BACK SEVEN TIMES WORSE

THE TRUTH...

The Bible does not teach that demons WILL come back in greater numbers and force, but that it is POSSIBLE for them to do so. It is true that we need to be wise as to whom we minister deliverance. How would a lost man have anything with which to fill his "house?" Therefore, based on this scripture (Matt. 12:43–45), deliverance is *only* for the believer in Jesus Christ and he or she has nothing to fear.

Furthermore, as mentioned, deliverance is "the children's bread" (Matt. 15:21–28; Mark 7:24–30). We should not fear partaking of deliverance-bread any more than we would in eating physical bread. Each are good for us!

OBSTACLE 8
DELIVERANCE MUST NEVER BE DONE IN PUBLIC

THE TRUTH...

Jesus consistently cast out evil spirits in public. There is no clear reference to private deliverance in His ministry. So, the scriptural pattern actually favors public ministry. We have witnessed miracles and breakthroughs in both public and in private. Both types of ministry are valid.

Furthermore, fear makes some people seek private deliverance. They have fear of demon manifestations, offending others, exposure of their private life and things getting out of control in general. The minister, likewise, may fear possible failure (nothing will happen), or fear his own exposure (something in himself brought to light).

OBSTACLE 9
DELIVERANCE IS JUST A MATTER OF FAITH

THE TRUTH...

By this some mean that if they have enough faith then God will automatically take care of all demons. But, God has given us authority and responsibility to deal with demons directly (Matt. 10:1; Luke 9:1; Mark 16:17).

It is true that faith is important to deliverance, for we must believe that when we speak to a demon it must obey. Demons know when we do not have faith and take advantage of it (Acts 19:13-17).

The disciples were unable to cast out a certain demon because of their unbelief. This implies that they were not to believe that the demon would just "go away," but that they could – and should – cast it out.

It is also the case, according to Jesus, that fasting and prayer builds faith to cast out demons (Matt. 17:14-21).

"Faith, if it has no works, is dead" (Jas. 2:17). What is the meaning of this verse? The one who has active faith will be active in the world around him. Hence, he will be speaking to the "mountains" in his way.

Demonization should be considered a "mountain" to be removed by speaking in faith (Mark 11:22–23).

Passive faith is contrary to Scripture's command that we engage in warfare and "wrestle" against principalities and powers, "resist" the devil and "cast out" demons (Eph. 6:12, Jas. 4:7, Matt. 10:1).

Obstacle 10
Deliverance Must be With (or Without) Manifestations

The Truth...

There were manifestations when Jesus ministered deliverance. For example, a young man was thrown to the ground as though having a seizure; a demon spoke through a man in the synagogue; and spirits cried in loud voices (Lk. 9:39; Mk. 1:26; 9:20,26). Therefore, we should not expect all manifestations to be eliminated.

However, there are often *unnecessary* manifestations. Demons will manifest when given the opportunity. They are prideful beings, and they enjoy attention. In spiritism, for instance, demons manifest because they are given permission, and manifestations are sought. The same will occur in deliverance when demon manifestations are courted. The goal of deliverance is not to get demons to manifest but to cast them out!

Manifestations are not the criteria for judging the validity of deliverance. *Peace* and *freedom from bondage* are the earmarks of successful deliverance. Manifestations should not be sought or required.

OBSTACLE 11
DEMONOLOGY AND DELIVERANCE GLORIFY THE DEVIL, WE SHOULD KEEP OUR MINDS ON JESUS

THE TRUTH...

This sounds good, but it is false reasoning. The Bible does not teach us to ignore the devil but to confront, resist, wrestle, stand against and cast him out (Eph. 6:12).

Jesus is glorified when we are engaged in spiritual warfare because we are exalting His Name, His precious blood and His Word. We often battle with praise and worship. We also battle through fasting and prayer. Most of all, we battle through the ministry of deliverance. Satan gets no glory through being defeated. All the glory goes to the One who is stronger than the devil, and the devil is humiliated when his house is spoiled.

OBSTACLE 12
THOSE WHO GET INVOLVED IN DELIVERANCE SUFFER PERSONAL ATTACKS FROM THE DEVIL

THE TRUTH...

This error has actually been promoted by a few ministers of deliverance. Sometimes ministers wrestle against flesh and blood and get wounded. As is always the case, wisdom and discernment are needed when battling the enemy. Thankfully, this why we have the Holy Spirit.

To say that demons can retaliate is contrary to Luke 10:19. We can tread upon serpents and scorpions, and they can in no way harm us.

This obstacle has a way of becoming a self-fulfilling prophecy. If the deliverance minister is fearful or doubts his own authority it will give demons grounds to attack him. Fear is to be soundly defeated on all grounds.

We are equipped with "the whole armor of God" (Eph. 6:11). If one is wounded in spiritual battle he should check his armor to be sure it is all in place.

OBSTACLE 13
JESUS DID IT ALL FOR US — WE DON'T NEED TO FIGHT

THE TRUTH...

The devil would like for us to adopt this position. It would mean that he could work against us without challenge.

We very much agree that a person can become too demon-conscious. We are to be *Jesus-conscious*, and rejoice because our names are written in heaven (Luke 10:20).

There is widespread misunderstanding as to what is meant by Jesus defeating the devil. Jesus did not destroy the devil; he destroyed the "works" of the devil (1 John 3:8). The devil has not yet been chained and put into the bottomless pit. He is still "roaming about" (1 Pet. 5:8). He remains the "god of this world" (2 Cor 4:4), where he rules as "the prince of the power of the air" (Eph. 2:2). The Church has been commissioned to destroy him in his "gates" (Matt 16:18).

CONCLUSION

There was once a man in the synagogue who had a demon. When Jesus cast the demon out, it caused much questioning among the people. They asked, "What is this? What new doctrine is this?" (Mark 1:27).

Today, these same questions, and others, come up when deliverance is taught or witnessed. Jesus patiently answered the inquiries of those who were sincere, but He did not allow Himself to be pulled into debate by those who were obstinate and unteachable.

The teaching given here is with the prayer and hope that any whose unsettled questions have prevented his involvement in deliverance will now be able to go forth in obedience to the Lord. God has not called us to debate deliverance but to do it! For ...

"THESE SIGNS SHALL FOLLOW THEM THAT BELIEVE;
IN MY NAME SHALL THEY CAST OUT DEMONS..."

MARK 16:17

Other Books & Booklets
by Frank & Ida Mae Hammond

Books

Pigs in the Parlor	$10.95
STUDY GUIDE: Pigs in the Parlor	$9.95
The Breaking of Curses	$8.95
Overcoming Rejection	$8.95
A Manual for Children's Deliverance	$9.95
Demons & Deliverance	$10.95
Kingdom Living for the Family	$9.95
Saints at War: Spiritual Warfare over Territories	$6.95
Comfort for the Wounded Spirit	$6.95

Booklets

Confronting Familiar Spirits	$5.95
The Father's Blessing	$5.95
Forgiving Others	$5.95
God Warns America: Arise Oh Church!	$5.95
The Marriage Bed	$5.95
Obstacles to Deliverance & Why Deliverance Sometimes Fails	$5.95
Our Warfare	$5.95
Perils of Passivity	$5.95
Promoted by God	$5.95
Repercussions from Sexual Sins	$5.95
Soul Ties	$5.95
The Strongman of Unbelief	$5.95
The Tales of Two Franks	$5.95

Compact Discs (6 CDs Each)

The Deliverance Series	$29.95	Walk in the Spirit	$29.95
Freedom from Bondage	$29.95	The Family Series	$29.95
The End-Time Series	$29.95	The Church Series	$29.95
The Faith Series	$29.95	Spiritual Meat Series	$29.95

FRANK HAMMOND BOOKS

PIGS IN THE PARLOR

A handbook for deliverance from demons and spiritual oppression. Frank Hammond explains the practical application of the ministry of deliverance, patterned after the ministry of Jesus Christ. With over 1 million copies in print worldwide, and translated into more than a dozen languages, Pigs in the Parlor remains the authoritative book on the subject of deliverance. *Also available in Spanish.*

STUDY GUIDE: PIGS IN THE PARLOR

A companion guide to help you dig deeper into this deliverance classic! Designed as a study tool for either individuals or groups. It will enable you to: diagnose your own, personal deliverance needs; walk you through the process of becoming free; equip you to set others free from demonic torment. This new Study Guide includes questions and answers on a chapter by chapter basis as well as new information to further your knowledge of deliverance.

OVERCOMING REJECTION

Frank Hammond addresses the all-too-common root problem of rejection and the fear of rejection in the lives of believers, and provides steps to be set free. Learn how past experiences can influence our actions, and how we can be made whole. Discover the various causes of rejection, including abuse, peer rejection, marriage rejection, Church rejection, and others.

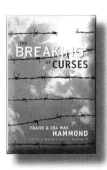

THE BREAKING OF CURSES

The Bible refers to curses over 230 times, and 70 sins that cause curses are put forth in Scripture. Learn how Curses are just as real today as in Biblical times. This book shows what curses are and how you may deliver yourself and your family from them.

Impact Christian Books
www.impactchristianbooks.com
1-800-451-2708

A MANUAL FOR CHILDREN'S DELIVERANCE

The Hammond's book for ministering to children, a valuable tool for parents to learn how to set their children free from spiritual bondages. Learn the basics of how to effectively minister deliverance to children. *Also available in Spanish.*

DEMONS & DELIVERANCE

This book sets forth guiding principles from Scripture and the ministry of Jesus for confronting demons and delivering the oppressed. You will learn discerning right & wrong methods of deliverance; the believer's commission & authority & being anointed; maintaining balance in deliverance; keeping out of the devil's reach, demonic connection with mental illness & disease, and more.

THE SAINTS AT WAR

The Hammond's book on waging spiritual warfare over territories, including cities and nation. Learn about warfare in the heavenlies, and how to pray for cities and for nations.

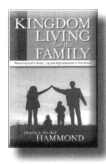

KINGDOM LIVING FOR THE FAMILY

Restoring God's Peace, Joy and Righteousness in the Home. God has a specific plan for your family, one that includes the peace, joy and righteousness of the Kingdom of God. However, too many families have settled for much less than what God has provided. You will gain insights into: The root causes of common problems in marriage, Spiritual warfare in the family, Scriptural guidance on the roles of husbands and wives, Bringing up children in the Lord, and more!

Other Frank Hammond Books & Booklets

Soul Ties

A Frank Hammond Booklet. A discussion of various types of good & bad soul ties. Good ties covered include marriage, friendship, parent/child, between christians. bad ties include those formed from fornication, evil companions, perverted family ties, with the dead, and demonic ties through the church.

Our Warfare

A Frank Hammond Booklet on Spiritual Warfare. In 2 Cor. 10, we are alerted that there is a war. Our war is a spiritual war. Our Commander in Chief has issued us the required weaponry and has given His name as our authority. Let us take up our warfare and defeat the enemy!

The Marriage Bed

A Frank Hammond Booklet. Can the marriage bed be defiled? The author provides helpful advice on how to keep the Marriage Bed pure before the Lord. Drawing from God's emphasis on purity and holiness in our lives, the booklet explains how to avoid perverse sexual demonic activity in a home.

Forgiving Others

A Frank Hammond Booklet. Unforgiveness brings a curse, and can be a major roadblock to the deliverance and freedom of your soul. Find the spiritual truths regarding the necessity of forgiveness and the blessings of inner freedom which result! Find out why "70 times 7" is for our benefit as much as for the people we forgive.

Impact Christian Books
www.impactchristianbooks.com
1-800-451-2708

Miraculous Testimonies
of Spiritual Warfare!

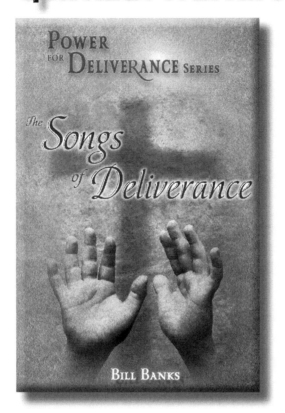

Power for Deliverance (Songs of Deliverance)
by Bill Banks

From over 30 years of counseling and ministering deliverance, Bill Banks highlights the common root causes of emotional and mental torment, and walks the reader through steps to be set free. Includes revelations from 17 people delivered from various trauma and torment.

This book shows that there is help for oppressed, tormented and compulsive people, and that the solution is as old as the ministry of Jesus Christ!

Impact Christian Books
www.impactchristianbooks.com
1-800-451-2708

Impact Christian Books

These books are available through your local bookstore,
or you may order directly from
Impact Christian Books.

Website: www.impactchristianbooks.com

Phone Order Line: **1-800-451-2708**
(314)-822-3309

Address: **Impact Christian Books**
332 Leffingwell Ave. Suite #101
Kirkwood, MO 63122

- You may also request a free Catalog -

2223302R20017

Made in the USA
San Bernardino, CA
26 March 2013